THE PROFITABLE TRADER

PART 1

"A MUST HAVE IN EVERY CLOSET"

NITIN SINGLA

BLUEROSE PUBLISHERS
India | U.K.

Copyright © Nitin Singla 2024

All rights reserved by author. No part of this publication may be reproduced, stored in a retrieval system or transmitted in any form or by any means, electronic, mechanical, photocopying, recording or otherwise, without the prior permission of the author. Although every precaution has been taken to verify the accuracy of the information contained herein, the publisher assume no responsibility for any errors or omissions. No liability is assumed for damages that may result from the use of information contained within.

BlueRose Publishers takes no responsibility for any damages, losses, or liabilities that may arise from the use or misuse of the information, products, or services provided in this publication.

For permissions requests or inquiries regarding this publication,
please contact:

BLUEROSE PUBLISHERS
www.BlueRoseONE.com
info@bluerosepublishers.com
+91 8882 898 898
+4407342408967

ISBN: 978-93-6783-076-5

Cover design: Daksh
Typesetting: Tanya Raj Upadhyay

First Edition: October 2024

About the Author

Nitin Singla, by profession, is a Solution architect with an IT company. He belongs from a town Ladwa which falls under Distt. Kurukshetra, Haryana

Investing and trading came into his life as a hobby which he is still learning and working on day by day to hone his trading skills.

According to the author it takes years to learn trading skills and the content out in the market is either too complex for anyone to understand or it's been focused only to a specific kind of people.

By this book and the series of books which will come, author will try his sincere efforts to make you a better trader, better each passing day. Author also believes in perfect practise bring perfect results.

Author doesn't know at what stage of your trading journey you are into. So, with this book will start with the vary basics and we learn and grow further with more books and content.

Let's say "radhe radhe". Krishan ji kehte hai, jo hua, acha hua, jo ho rha hai, acha hi ho rha hai and jo hoga acha hi hoga.

With a positive mindset I will start writing and with a positive mindset you will start reading this book and worship gods and goddesses to get their blessing in so called trading journey.

Below are my social handles:

Instagram: nitin.singla.86, profitabletrader09

Gmail: 09nitinsingla@gmail.com

Table of Contents

Introduction 1
    Overview of the stock market 1
    My journey and experiences 14

Understanding the Basics 18
    Key concepts (stocks, bonds, market indices) 18
    Explanation of market dynamics 21

What to do: Strategies for success 24
    Researching stocks: 24
    Analysing /market trends 33
    Diversification Tips: 37

What not to do: Common pitfalls 39
    Emotional Trading 41
    Ignoring market signals 49
    Overtrading 52

Risk Management 62
    Position Sizing: 67
    Risk/reward ratio 68

Real - Life examples: **71**
   Case studies of successful trades and lessons from losses: 71
   Personal anecdotes 74

Conclusion **78**
   Encouragement and concluding thoughts: 78

What's Coming Next **80**

Introduction

Overview of the stock market

A **stock market**, **equity market**, or **share market** is the aggregation of buyers and sellers of stocks (also called shares). In other words, the stock market is a platform where investors buy and sell shares of publicly traded companies. It serves as a crucial component of the global economy, facilitating capital allocation and providing companies with access to funding.

Key Concepts

1. **Stocks**: Ownership stakes in a company. When you buy a share, you own a small piece of that company.

2. **Exchanges**: Places where stocks are bought and sold, such as the New York Stock Exchange (NYSE) or NSE (National Stock Exchange) for India. A stock exchange is an exchange (or

bourse) where stockbrokers and traders can buy and sell shares (equity stock), bonds, and other securities. Many large companies have their stocks listed on a stock exchange.

3. **Indices**: Benchmarks that track the performance of a group of stocks, like the S&P 500, Nifty 50, Bank Nifty, CNXIT, others.

4. **Market Capitalization**: The total market value of a company's outstanding shares, indicating its size.

5. **Bull and Bear Markets**: A bull market indicates rising prices and investor confidence, while a bear market signifies falling prices and pessimism. While a lot of times, a user is confused whether it's a bull market or bear market. It can be bull market checking on a particular timeframe and can appear to be a bear market on a different timeframe. Always, analyse on higher

timeframe first before analysing on smaller timeframe.

As we discussed earlier, the stock market is an electronic marketplace. Buyers and sellers electronically express their points of view in terms of trade.

For example, consider the current situation of Infosys. When writing this, Infosys faces a management succession issue, and most of the company's senior-level executives are resigning. The leadership vacuum is weighing down the company's reputation heavily. As a result, the stock price dropped to Rs.3,000 from Rs.3,500.

Assume there are two traders – A and B.

A's view on Infosys – The stock price will go down further because the company will find it challenging to find a new CEO. If A trades from his point of view, he should be a seller of the Infosys stock.

However, B views the same situation differently and has a different point of view.

According to her, the stock price of Infosys has overreacted to the succession issue, and soon the company will find a great leader. The stock price will eventually move up.

If B trades from her point of view, she should be a buyer of the Infosys stock.

So, at, Rs.3000, A will be a seller, and B will be a buyer in Infosys.

Now both A and B will place orders to sell and buy the stocks respectively through their respective stockbrokers. The stockbroker routes it to the stock exchange. The stock exchange must ensure that these two orders are matched and that the trade is executed. This is the primary job of the stock market – to facilitate the transactions between different market participants.

A stock market is where market participants can access any publicly listed company and trade from their point of view if other participants have an opposing point of view or similar.

What moves the stock?

Let us continue with the Infosys example to understand how stocks move. Imagine you are a market participant tracking Infosys.

It is 10:00 AM Infosys is trading at Rs.3000 per share. The management makes a press statement that they have found a new CEO expected to steer the company to greater heights. They are confident that the newly appointed CEO will do good things for the company.

Two questions –

a) How will the stock price of Infosys react to this news?
b) If you were to place a trade on Infosys, what would it be? Would it be a buy or a sell?

The answer to the first question is quite simple; the news is positive, so the stock price will increase. Infosys had a leadership issue, and the company has fixed it. When positive announcements are made, market participants tend to buy the stock at any given price, which cascades into a stock price rally.

Let me illustrate this further:

Sl No	Time	Last Traded Price	What price the seller wants	What does the buyer do?	New Last Trade Price
01	10:00	3000	3002	Buys	3002
02	10:01	3002	3006	Buys	3006
03	10:03	3006	3011	Buys	3011
04	10:05	3011	3016	Buys	3016

Notice that the buyer is willing to pay whatever prices the seller wants; this is when the market is said to be bullish. In a bullish market, the prices tend to move up.

So, as you can see, the stock price jumped 16 Rupees in a matter of 5 minutes. Though this is a fictional situation, it is a realistic and typical behaviour of stocks. The stock price increases when the news is good or expected to be good.

In this case, the stock moves up because of two reasons. One, the leadership issue has been fixed, and two, there is also an expectation that the new CEO will steer the company to greater heights.

The answer to the second question is now quite simple; you buy Infosys stocks because there is good news surrounding the stock.

Now, moving forward on the same day, at 12:30 PM, 'The National Association of Software & Services company' (NASSCOM) makes a statement stating that the customer's IT budget seems to have come down by 15%, which could have an impact on the industry in the future. For those unaware, NASSCOM is a trade association of Indian IT companies.

By 12:30 PM, let us assume Infosys is trading at 3030. Few questions for you…

a) How does this new information impact Infosys?

b) What would it be if you were to initiate a new trade with this information?
c) What would happen to the other IT stocks in the market?

The answers to the above questions are quite simple. Before we answer these questions, let us analyse NASSCOM's statement in more detail.

NASSCOM says that the IT budget is likely to shrink by 15%. This means IT companies' revenues and profits will go down soon. This is not great news for the IT industry.

Let us now try and answer the above questions…

a) Infosys is a leading IT major in the country and will react to this news. The reaction could be mixed because there was good news specific to Infosys earlier during the day. However, a 15% decline in revenue is a serious matter, and hence Infosys stocks are likely to trade lower.

b) At 3030, if one were to initiate a new trade based on the new information, it would be a sell on Infosys.

c) The information released by NASSCOM applies to the entire IT stocks and not just Infosys. Hence all IT companies are likely to witness selling pressure.

So, as you notice, market participants react to news and events, and their reaction translates to price movements! This is what makes the stocks move.

At this stage, you may wonder what would happen to a company's share price if there were no news. Will the stock price stay flat and not move at all? The answer is yes and no, depending on the company in focus.

For example, let us assume there is no news concerning two different companies…

1) Reliance Industries Limited
2) Shree Lakshmi Sugar Mills

As we all know, Reliance is one the largest companies in the country, and regardless of whether there is news or not, market participants would like to buy or sell the company's shares, and therefore the price moves constantly.

The second company is unknown and, therefore, may not attract market participants' attention as there is no news or event surrounding this company. Under such circumstances, the stock price may not move, or even if it does, it may be very marginal.

To summarize, the price moves because of expectations of news and events. The news or events can be related to the company, industry, or the economy. For instance, the appointment of Narendra Modi as the Indian Prime Minister was perceived as positive news, and therefore the whole stock market moved.

In some cases, there would be no news, but still, the price could move due to the demand and supply situation.

How does the stock get traded?

You have decided to buy 200 shares of Infosys at 3030 and hold on to it for one year. How does it work? What is the exact process of buying the stock? What happens after you buy it?

Systems work seamlessly to ensure your transactions go smoothly.

With your decision to buy Infosys, you need to log in to your trading account (provided by your stockbroker) and place an order to buy Infosys. Once you place an order, the following details are validated –

1. Details of your trading account through which you intend to buy Infosys shares.
2. The price at which you intend to buy Infosys.
3. The number of shares you intend to buy.

Before your broker transmits this order to the exchange, the broker must ensure you have sufficient money to buy these shares. If yes, then this order hits the stock exchange. Once the order hits the market, the stock exchange (through their order matching algorithm) tries to find a seller who is willing to sell you 200 shares of Infosys at 3030.

Now the seller could be one person willing to sell the entire 200 shares at 3030, or it could be ten people selling 20 shares each, or two people selling 1 and 199 shares, respectively. The permutation and combination do not matter. From your perspective, all you need is 200 shares of Infosys at 3030, and you have placed an order for the same. The stock exchange ensures the shares are available to you if sellers are in the market.

Once the trade is executed, the shares will be electronically credited to your DEMAT account. Likewise, the shares will be electronically debited from the seller's DEMAT account.

What happens after you own stock?

After you buy the shares, the shares will reside in your DEMAT account. You are now a part owner of the company to the extent of your shareholding.

By owning the shares, you are entitled to corporate benefits like dividends, stock splits, bonuses, rights issues, voting rights, etc.

A note on the holding period

The holding period is the period you intend to hold the stock. You may be surprised that the holding period could be as short as a few minutes to as long as 'forever.'

Depends on what kind of trader you and what your mindset was when you bought the stock, your holding period will be. If you took a trade on the fundamental analysis which looks very strong to you and you won't sell it until the stock doubles, then that's your target or if trade was taken entirely based on technical analysis (reading charts), then targets should be as per certain tools and techniques which can be used to conclude targets or charts.

My journey and experiences

It has been a great learning journey so far.

I remember the very initial time; I jumped into trading and realised it could be a medium to make money. After I read a little about it which was all so confusing already, like seeing the chart first time on a platform like trading view, it was like what the f**k is that, is it called a chart and there's way to read it and make money? Really? As I read about it increasingly, I got to know there are these candlesticks, the building blocks of a chart and the very next moment I ordered a book online to learn more about these candlesticks and candlestick chart patterns to make myself learn candlestick chart patterns. The book talked about the various candlesticks like a DOJI candle, a hammer, hanging man or patterns like morning star and evening star. The guy who wrote the book, suggested to use candlestick patten with a particular Indicator (you can find a lots of indicators under Indicators section on trading view). That was it, I thought, I am now king of the market understanding how the market works, and I am going to make hell lot of money from the market using these candlestick patterns. To my surprise, there's always some or the candlestick forming making me rethink my decision of whether to take a trade or not. Some trades worked and some didn't, and I started having a feeling that I have lost in the game of trading. For a go-getter, who keeps fighting, this sad feeling of losing in the game wasn't at all a good start. As I trade now, I don't see at all what kind of candlestick is getting formed and what juncture in the price chart because I have seen candlesticks failing so many times, where they could have worked. So, for me formation of a particular type of candlestick doesn't matter at all, I just don't use them. If it's working for some of you and giving good results in a particular strategy, I will be happy to know about it and I will love to test it myself also. Please write to my email.

I was done with candlesticks, and that didn't work well with me. So, if not candlesticks what else I can learn and benefit from this market I thought?

There I came across patterns; symmetrical triangle pattern, ascending and descending triangle patterns, head and shoulders, inverse head and shoulders pattern, cup and handle, bullish and bearish pennants and flags and many others.

Got fully excited, that looks like I got the nerve, these are some pre-documented patterns in some high ranked books and some highly ranked websites. Started concentrating only on such patterns and tried finding them on different timeframes. To my surprise, again some of these worked and some of these didn't. I felt like I am back where I started, with me again losing so much of time and energy gaining something which I found out was only a very little of value to my now.

What did I need next?

As I believed that I'm go-getter, I thought I should concentrate on my decent paying job and personal relationships and other interests but the fact that there's something huge to make money from market was again keeping me restless and I went on rest for some days in introspection.

Started with the new energy and followed 2-3 YouTube channels which used to give crypto related buy/sell calls. As I proceeded with their content and other videos, I noticed they also were using the same concepts of triangles, head, and shoulders, which didn't go very well with me. If something has a very low percentage of win rate, then that's nothing but pure gambling.

I never myself saw stock or crypto market as gambling but a market to make money.

Understanding the Basics

Key concepts (stocks, bonds, market indices)

a) **Stocks**: Ownership stakes in a company. When you buy a share, you own a small piece of that company. It's already explained in a detailed manner in Chapter 1.

b) **Bonds**: A bond is a type of investment security that allows an investor to lend money to a company or government in exchange for interest payments and the return of the principal amount when the bond matures. Bonds are considered fixed-income investments because they provide a steady stream of income over the life of the bond.

Here are some things to know about bonds:

a) How they work

When an investor buys a bond, they are lending money to the issuer, who can be a company, government, or municipality. The issuer agrees to pay the investor interest at a specified rate and return the principal amount when the bond matures.

b) Why they are important.

Bonds can be a key part of a diversified investment portfolio, as they can help reduce the risk of short-term losses. They can also provide a steady income during retirement.

c) How to avoid fraud

When investing in bonds, it's important to be aware of potential fraud.

c) **Market Indices:** A stock market index measures the performance of a group of stocks. It represents a specific segment of the market, such as large companies or sectors. A stock market index helps investors track market trends, compare investments, and make informed decisions without focusing on individual stock movements.

Index prices are influenced by various factors, including economic indicators (like GDP growth and inflation), corporate earnings reports, interest rates, geopolitical events, and market sentiment. Changes in these factors can cause significant movements in the index, reflecting the overall market performance.

The three major indices in the Indian stock market are the Sensex, Nifty, and Nifty Bank. Sensex and Nifty track the performance of large-cap companies, while Nifty Bank focuses on the banking sector. These indices provide insights into the overall market trends and specific sectors.

Popular tradable indices include Nifty 50 and Nifty Bank. Investors can trade these indices through index futures and options, which are financial derivatives based on the indices.

Explanation of market dynamics

Market dynamics are forces that will impact prices and the behaviours. In a market, these forces create pricing signals that result from the fluctuation of supply and demand for a given product or service.

Before we look more specifically at market dynamics, let's touch on supply and demand. Supply and demand fundamentals form the cornerstone of market dynamics. The relationship between the quantity of a good or service that producers are willing to supply and the quantity that consumers are willing to purchase at various price points creates a market, and the forces that change each of those are the market dynamics.

Below takes us further to the relationship between supply and demand. As we see in below chart, as Supply increases, price also increases and as demand decreases price also decreases. There will be a point between Supply and Demand levels called Equilibrium levels.

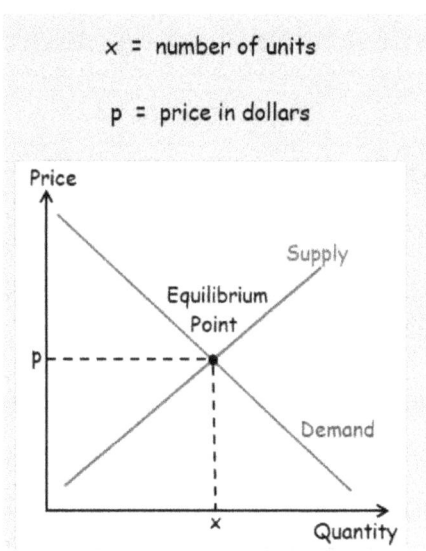

Also called a market-clearing price, the equilibrium price is that at which demand matches supply, producing a market equilibrium that's acceptable to buyers and sellers.

Supply and demand in terms of the quantity of the goods are balanced at the point where an upward-sloping supply curve and a downward-sloping demand curve intersect leaving no surplus supply or unmet demand.

Apple's supply and demand management team helps achieve financial and sales goals by forecasting demand and driving supply. Their work includes:

- Demand forecasting: Developing forecasts to support planning and activities such as factory builds and customer allocation

- Supply planning: Driving manufacturing capacity and materials purchase requirements

- New product introduction (NPI): Ensuring customers receive products on time through all sales channels

What to do: Strategies for success

Researching stocks:

To research for projects/companies to choose for, either choose projects which are trading at or below their equilibrium price or which recently did a breakout at their levels according to high time frames.

To understand all that we must first understand first, how a candle looks like and how to read a chart.

A bullish and Bearish candle will look like below. Notice and remember the various terms being used:

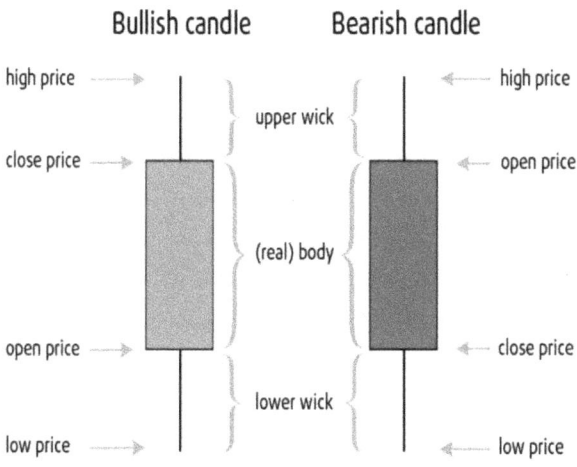

Here, consider 1st candle as the Bullish Green candle and second candle as the Bearish Red candle.

Green colour for a Bullish candle and red for a bearish one is highly used globally. You can use colours as per you in setting of tools like Trading view. Also, accustom yourself to using trading view or some tool like that to plot charts and indicators and to analyse further.

Swing lows and Swing Highs

Swing Lows: A combination of three candles with lower price of middle candle lower than lower price of both in candle in front and following

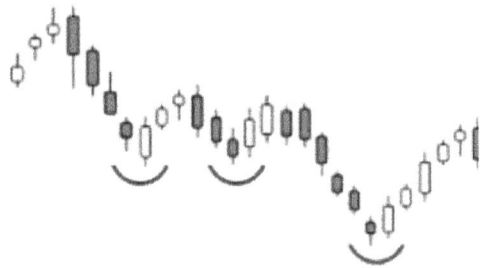

Definition:

A Swing Low is a 'valley' identified within a series of bars or within an indicator or oscillator. A Swing Low consists of two "legs" and starts with an initial down leg which is then followed by an up leg. A leg is defined as two or more bars going in any one direction. For example, when two or more consecutive bars produce lower (bar) highs and lower (bar) lows. In this instance, the smallest possible down leg would have developed. Inversely, to have an up leg you need no fewer than two bars showing higher (bar) highs and higher (bar) lows. When a down leg is followed by an up leg, the valley that is created is considered a Swing Low.

Background: A Swing Low starts its life out as a pivot low consisting of a high low to the left and right of a price bar. To additionally produce a formal Swing Low requires that the bar forming the price low has two bars with higher lows preceding it and two bars with higher lows following it.

Swing Lows can act as an area of support or resistance.

Practical use: Defining a Swing Low is helpful to technical analysts because many trendlines are drawn connecting the peaks of Swing Lows to each other. This is also helpful to begin gaining a deeper understanding of the sentiment read of a chart.

Swing Highs: A combination of three candles with higher price of middle candle higher than higher price of both in candle in front and following

Swing Highs

Definition:

A Swing High is a "peak" identified within a series of bars or within an indicator or oscillator. A Swing High consists of two "legs" and starts with an initial up leg which is then followed by a down leg. A leg is defined as two or more bars going in any one direction. For example, when two or more consecutive bars produce higher (bar) highs and higher (bar) lows. In this instance, the smallest possible up leg would have developed. Inversely, to have a down leg you need no fewer than two bars showing lower (bar) highs and lower (bar) lows. When an up leg is followed by a down leg, the "peak" that is created is considered a Swing High.

Background: A Swing High starts its life out as a pivot high consisting of a lower high to the left and right of a price bar. To additionally produce a formal Swing High requires that the bar forming the price high has two bars with lower highs preceding it and two bars with lower highs following it.

Practical Use: Defining a Swing High is helpful to technical analysts because many trendlines are drawn connecting the peaks of Swing Highs to each other. This is also helpful to begin gaining a deeper understanding of the sentiment read of a char.

Dealing range:

To understand the concept of Equilibrium, lets understand the concept of Dealing Range once. Dealing range is formed or constructed using Swing highs and swing low.

We will use Fib Retracement tool in trading view to check how much % price has retraced. Consider, below example of a chart of Bosch Ltd.

D1 and D2 are Swing highs and swing lows here. And the range between them constituting a dealing range.

Now, apply Fib retracement tool from left bar to the graph between points D1 and D2.

See in below chart, how price went below 50% level which was equilibrium. Actually, went till 0.786 level which is a golden zone to buy, obviously much cheaper and better price to buy then at Equilibrium price but the point is if price moves back from 0.5 level, then also, we can't say that price isn't obeying the levels because 0.5 level or Equilibrium level was met.

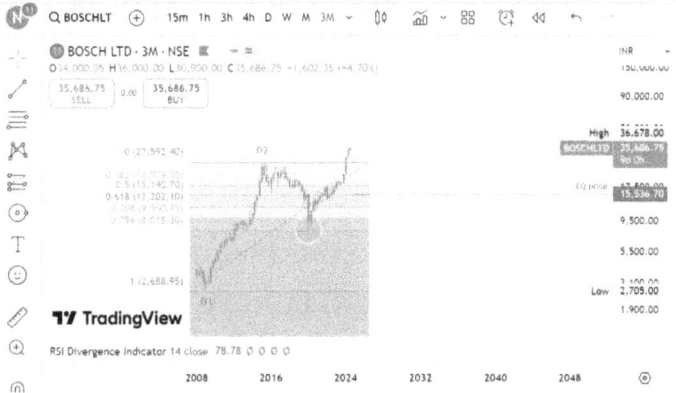

Now, as we have already discussed about Fibonacci Retracement, let's discuss that in little more detail.

Fibonacci retracement levels are prices, depicted as horizontal lines on a chart, that indicate where support or resistance could likely to occur.

Each price level is associated with a percentage amount that measures how much of a retracement has occurred from a prior peak in the price action. The retracement amounts are based on numbers identified in a Fibonacci sequence. The Fibonacci retracement levels are 23.6%, 38.2%, 61.8%, and 78.6%. While not officially a Fibonacci ratio, 50% is also used.

The indicator is useful because it can be drawn between any two significant price points, such as a high and a low. The indicator will then create the levels between those two points.

Look at below chart of Crompton Greaves:

After making a swing high around 294, it retraced to .708 Fibonacci level before making a new high. Equilibrium for this chart was around 209.

More about Fibonacci, its retracements, extensions to determine the price targets will cover in next series of books.

Analysing /market trends

Trend is the direction that prices are moving in, based on where they have been in the past. Trends are made up of peaks and troughs. It is the direction of those peaks and troughs that constitute a market's trend. Whether those peaks and troughs are moving up, down, or sideways indicates the direction of the trend.

- An asset or a market that experiences an overall price increase over a certain period is said to be in an uptrend or a bull market.

- When an asset's price moves into a series of lower highs and lower lows, it's said to be in a downtrend or bear market.

- Market trends help traders and investors in identifying trading opportunities.

How does a market trend work?

To understand what market trend, mean, it's important to note what factors may shape one.

- **Government policy**

Using fiscal and monetary policy, governments can slow or accelerate the growth of market trends. For example, adjusting a central bank's interest rate could affect a country's economic growth, having a direct impact on cyclical and defensive sectors.

- **Market sentiment**

Market trends can be shaped by the sentiment among market participants. When traders and investors have faith in the direction of a country's economy or a company's business outlook, their optimistic attitude can shape a bullish trend. On the contrary, a negative market sentiment among traders can push the asset's price lower.

- **Supply and demand**

The asset price tends to fluctuate following shifts in dynamics between supply and demand. This is especially relevant for commodities. For example, when the economy is booming, demand for crude oil rises, oil prices tend to rise. Wars and mining disruptions restrict supply, therefore too boosting the prices.

- **Corporate and economics news**

Upbeat results in company quarterly reports or positive economic readings that beat expectations can all contribute to an uptrend. On the contrary, negative news could push prices lower, creating a downtrend.

Uptrend:

Below chart will be referred to as a stock in uptrend. Way of entries will be on basis if fib retracement or breakout (that will cover in future books)

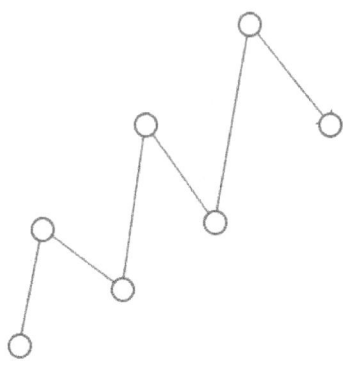

Here, as we can see, market is making higher lows and higher highs in each iteration.

Downtrend:

Below chart will be referred to as a stock in downtrend. Way of entries will be on basis if fib retracement or breakdown (that will cover in future books)

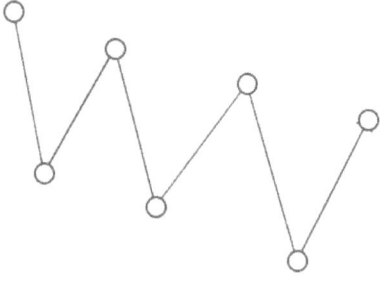

Notice, lower highs and lowers lows are being formed moving the price downwards continuously.

Sideways:

Below chart will be referred to as a stock in sideways trend. When market is in sideways trend, it means there's no clear trend until the price breakout in either of the directions.

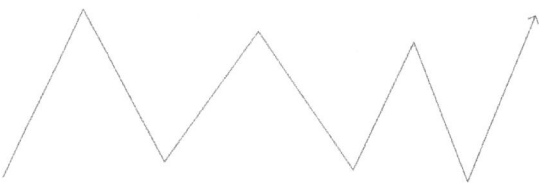

Notice, price is ranging between the same dealing range it created at first and clear breakouts have been noticed yet. So, the price is in sideways market.

Diversification Tips:

This topic might appear as little out of context here but is important to include. Stock market is a zero-sum game when you win someone loose. As they say, never put all your eggs in a basket, same concept applies here in Stock market also. Never put everything you have in a particular stock, or index or a particular category of stocks. It's not the end of the world, you might feel sometimes that there are 98% chances that this trade will work, still we never trade taking such a big position which can hamper with our personal well-being. We aren't here for gambling but for some serious business.

What not to do: Common pitfalls

When we are new to trading, we keep looking at the position repeatedly. We keep checking out PNL (Profit and Loss) every minute thereby disturbing our peace of mind which further leads to taking wrong trades.

As I mentioned earlier also, we must take trading as a serious business and refrain from getting ourselves attached to a company or a trade. As a trader, we must find a good trade and exit at take target levels or at Stop Loss whichever hits first. It shouldn't come to us that this trade came out as bad trade, now I will take a winning trade from this stock only and let's see who will win.

Always remember, that market is supreme, and we are just retail traders. Now comes the question not everyone is a retail trader? What do I mean by that?

Institutional Investor:

An institutional investor is an entity that makes investment decisions on behalf of individual members or shareholders. These investors typically trade 10,000 or more shares at a time and only engage in large transactions with large sums of money. E.g., banks

While complex investments in smaller companies are off limits to institutional investors, they have access to an investment benchmark that is not available to retail investors. For example, because of their huge pool of capital, institutions might invest in assets like commercial real estate, currencies, and futures.

Institutional investors are the ones which drive the market.

Retail Investors:

People like you; me and every commoner falls under this category. We are very small compared to institutional investors and we can't move a single candle. All we do is find a way and take entries were based on our experience that an institutional Investor could also be taking an entry. So, in a way we just copy them and take buy or sell calls at points where Institutional investors could be buying and selling, simple right? 😊 If you have enough experience in the market, could be else most of the times market is going to take money from you.

We were discussing about Emotional trading, lets jump back to that.

Emotional Trading

So, as I was discussing, we never have to attach our emotions with trading either winnings or losses. We must do trading like it's our primary business and we have invested in it to reap some fruits with it with time, obviously there will be seeds which will never convert to fruits and some overripen ones say the one's we didn't take profits at the right levels. But this is what it is!

Simply put, emotional trading is when a trader allows their psychological state to overpower a trading plan and divert from their rules. This can occur in multiple variations, such as but not limited to: Fear, greed, impatience, overconfidence, FOMO (Fear of moving out), etc.

It is quite normal to succumb to these emotions and make errors in trades as a beginner. The important thing is to learn from these mistakes (easier said than done) and learn thy self and overcome unpleasant habits like for example moving a stoploss further or pulling out of a winning trade at the first pullback just to see it rip to your TP shortly after. Some will be stubborn and narrow sighted, and it will take a lot longer to learn from their mistakes (that they might not even acknowledge) than others.

It is not a matter of avoiding these emotions (we can't just shut them off like robots) but learning how to spot them at the start and control them, so they do not force a mistake.

Having a proven tested strategy with a positive expectancy (an edge) will inspire confidence in trader's mind and should aid in neutralizing inevitable emotions during trading.

Understanding Trading Psychology

Trading psychology can be associated with a few specific emotions and behaviours that are often catalysts for market trading. Conventional characterizations of emotionally driven behaviour in markets ascribe most emotional trading to either greed or fear.

Greed can be thought of as an excessive desire for wealth, so extreme that it sometimes clouds rationality and judgment. Greed can lead traders toward a variety of suboptimal behaviours. This may include making high-risk trades, buying shares of an untested company or technology just because it is going up in price rapidly, or buying shares without researching the underlying investment.

Additionally, greed may inspire investors to stay in profitable trades longer than is advisable to squeeze out extra profits or to take on large speculative positions. Greed is most apparent in the final phase of bull markets when speculation runs rampant and investors throw caution to the wind.

Below chart shows a market cycle going through divergent phases from disbelief to Euphoria to again anger and disbelief and the cycle repeats.

PSYCHOLOGY OF A MARKET CYCLE

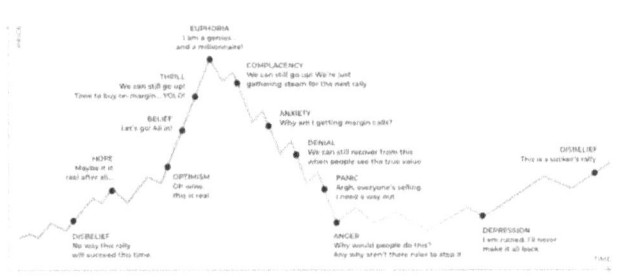

This shows that a market going up, will never keep going up ideally and will have some corrections on the way. Similarly, a market cycle going down will never keep going down and there will a SMS (shift in market structure) or BMS (breakout in market structure) upwards some hour/days of the week when the change will happen, and market trend will change to upwards.

SMS and BMS will study in next releases of this book.

Let's also understand key concepts of **Support and Resistance**.'

Support and resistance are two foundational concepts in technical analysis. Understanding what these terms mean, and their practical application is essential to correctly reading price charts.

Prices move because of supply and demand. When demand is greater than supply, prices rise. When supply is greater than demand, prices fall. Sometimes, prices will move sideways as both supply and demand are in equilibrium.

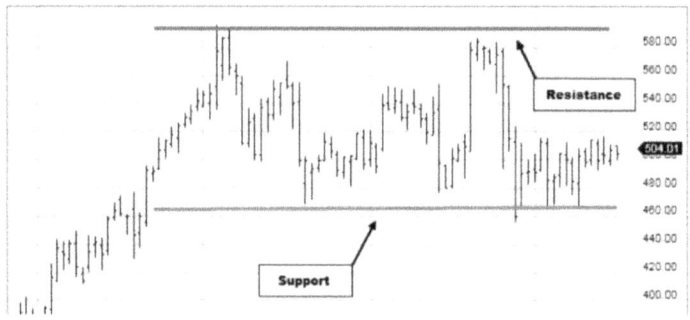

Support

Support is the level at which demand is strong enough to stop the stock from falling any further. In the image above you can see that each time the price reaches the support level, it has difficulty penetrating that level. The rationale is that as the price drops and approaches support, buyers (demand) become more inclined to buy, and sellers (supply) become less willing to sell.

Resistance

Resistance is the level at which supply is strong enough to stop the stock from moving higher. In the image above you can see that each time the price reaches the resistance level, it has a hard time moving higher. The rationale is that as the price rises and approaches resistance, sellers (supply) become more inclined to sell, and buyers (demand) become less willing to buy.

What creates support and resistance?

Think of supply and demand. When demand is greater than supply, prices tend to rise. When supply is greater than demand, prices tend to fall.

When there are more buyers than sellers (or when buyers are more aggressive), prices get bid up (as in an auction). Conversely, when there are more sellers than buyers (or when sellers are more aggressive), prices tend to get offered down.

But why might certain price levels—like support and resistance levels—attract an overwhelming level of buyers or sellers?

The simple answer is that traders and investors expect to see prices bounce at those levels for a variety of reasons. In most cases, these reasons are based on technical conditions and not economic or fundamental factors. Support and resistance become self-fulfilling prophecies based on trader psychology—in the short term, anyway. As time goes on, however, fundamental realities tend to outweigh the effects of chart-based expectations.

So, for investors, the question really is: "How can I identify potential support and resistance levels?

Example Of Resistance Becoming Support

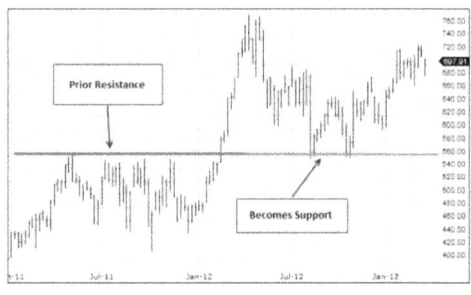

Here, in above case, once support is confirmed, one should look for opportunities using techniques like BMS in the same or little lower timeframes and target should be at least the last high and the subsequent highs would be derived by Fibonacci extensions. This will be studied in detail in next books to come.

As discussed in previous chapters, levels of fib retracements and extensions also wok as good levels of support and resistance.

Some other Resistance and Support Examples:

Ignoring market signals

Investors are always looking for ways to earn an edge in the markets. One area that is often overlooked is market sentiment.

While complex numbers and data are vital, understanding the prevailing sentiment can provide invaluable clues regarding where markets may be headed.

Ignoring market sentiment can be a risky approach for investors. This article will explore why paying attention to market sentiment is important and how to incorporate it into your investing strategy.

Market sentiment is important because it provides clues as to how investors are positioned. Extreme bullish or bearish sentiment can indicate the exhaustion of a trend.

If everyone is already fully invested, who is left to push the market higher? Conversely, when everyone is in panic mode, it may signal capitulation.

Besides, sentiment can serve as a contrarian indicator. Most investors are often wrong at extremes. When sentiment becomes overly euphoric, it may be time to start trimming positions or hedging. If investors are too fearful, it can present opportunities to buy at discounted prices.

"RSI divergence" is a good strategy to know about the tops and bottoms of the market.

Look at the below chart, we can notice there was a negative bearish divergence when Bitcoin made its high in Nov' 21 and was a good signal to exit the market.

Tools like RSI Divergence is a good tool to identify lows or highs in the market.

Below is a cheat sheet on how to use RSI divergence. More on RSI divergency divergence would be covered in books to come.

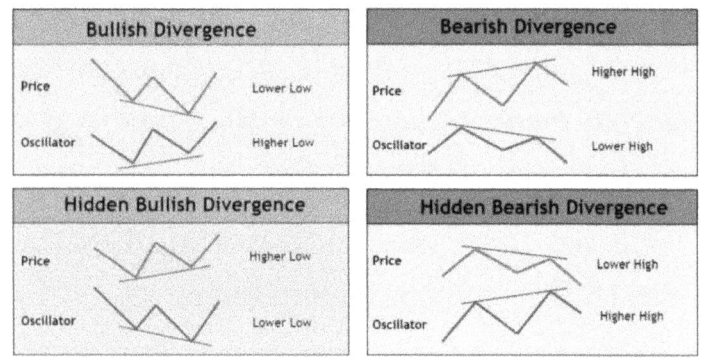

Overtrading

Overtrading refers to the excessive buying and selling of financial instruments, often driven by emotional and impulsive decisions rather than strategic analysis. This behaviour is characterised by frequent trades, high transaction volumes, and misusing a trading account.

Traders who overtrade typically do so to capitalise on short-term market movements, but this approach often backfires, leading to substantial financial losses.

What are the Problems Associated with Overtrading?

Overtrading can cause various problems for traders, both financially and psychologically. Understanding these issues is crucial to avoid falling into excessive trading. Here are the key issues associated with overtrading problems:

High Transaction Costs

Frequent trading increases transaction costs, including brokerage fees, taxes, and other charges. These costs can quickly erode profits, making it difficult for traders to achieve their financial goals. For instance, every trade executed incurs a fee, and when trades are numerous, these fees add up, significantly reducing the net gain from trading activities. Considering these costs when planning trading strategies is essential to ensure that expenses don't entirely consume profits.

Increased Risk

Overtrading exposes traders to higher risks. By taking numerous trades, traders may not have the time to conduct thorough research and analysis, leading to poor investment decisions and significant losses. When traders constantly enter and exit positions, they might miss critical information that could impact their decisions.

Emotional Stress

The pressure to constantly monitor the market and execute trades can cause emotional stress and fatigue. This stress can impair decision-making abilities, leading to further losses and a cycle of overtrading.

Traders may find themselves glued to their screens, trying to catch every market movement, which can be mentally exhausting and detrimental to their overall well-being. Managing emotional stress is crucial for maintaining a clear, focused mindset for successful trading.

Poor Portfolio Performance

Overtrading often results in suboptimal portfolio performance. Instead of holding on to high-quality investments for the long term, traders may frequently buy and sell, missing out on potential gains and compounding their losses.

This constant churning of the portfolio can prevent the investments from realising their full potential, as frequent trades may disrupt the growth trajectory of otherwise solid assets.

Capital Depletion

Continuous trading without a clear strategy can deplete trading capital. This not only affects current trading activities but also limits future profit opportunities. When capital is eroded due to excessive trading, it reduces the trader's ability to participate in new opportunities, thereby hindering long-term growth and profitability.

What are the Causes of Overtrading?

Understanding the causes of overtrading can help traders identify and address this behaviour. Here are some common factors that contribute to overtrading problems:

Lack of a Trading Plan

Many traders enter the stock market without a clear plan or strategy. They are likely to make impulsive decisions based on market fluctuations without a structured approach. A well-defined trading plan outlines specific goals, entry and exit points, and risk management strategies, which can help prevent impulsive trades driven by short-term market movements.

Emotional Trading

Emotions such as fear, greed, and excitement can drive traders to overtrade. For example, the fear of missing out (FOMO) can lead to impulsive buying, while panic can result in rapid selling. These emotional responses often override logical analysis, leading to poor trading decisions and increased risk. Recognising and managing these emotions is crucial to maintaining a disciplined trading approach.

Desire for Quick Profits

The allure of quick profits can tempt traders to execute numerous trades in a short period. However, this approach often overlooks the importance of thorough analysis and long-term planning. Chasing quick gains without proper research can result in significant losses, as impulsive trades are less likely to be based on solid analysis.

Overconfidence

Overconfident traders may believe they can consistently predict market movements and generate profits through frequent trading. This mindset can lead to excessive trading and significant losses. Overconfidence can cause traders to take on unnecessary risks and ignore potential warning signs, leading to detrimental outcomes.

Market Volatility

High market volatility can create an environment where traders feel compelled to react quickly to price changes. This reactive behaviour often results in overtrading. While volatility can present opportunities, it also increases the risk of making hasty decisions without considering the broader market context. Traders must learn to navigate volatility with a calm and measured approach.

How to Avoid Overtrading?

Avoiding overtrading requires a disciplined approach and a well-defined strategy. Here are some practical tips to help traders avoid the pitfalls of overtrading:

1. **Develop a Trading Plan**: Create a detailed trading plan that outlines your goals, risk tolerance, and strategies. Stick to this plan to avoid impulsive decisions.

2. **Set Limits**: Establish limits on the number of trades you execute within a specific period. This can help prevent excessive trading and promote more thoughtful decision-making.

3. **Focus on Quality**: Prioritise the quality of trades over quantity. Conduct thorough research and analysis to identify high-quality investment opportunities.

4. **Manage Emotions**: Recognise the impact of emotions on your trading decisions. Practice mindfulness and stress management techniques to maintain a calm and rational mindset.

5. **Review Performance**: Regularly review your trading performance to identify patterns of overtrading. Use this information to adjust your strategy and improve future outcomes.

6. **Exercise self-awareness:** Investors who are aware they may be overtrading can take actions to prevent it from occurring. Frequent assessments of trading activity can reveal patterns that suggest an investor may be overtrading. For instance, a progressive increase in

the number of trades each month may be a telltale sign of the problem.

7. **Take a break:** Overtrading may be caused by investors feeling as though they must make a trade. This often results in less-than-optimal trades being taken that result in a loss. Taking time off from trading allows investors to reassess their trading strategies and ensure they fit their overall investment objectives.

8. **Create rules:** Adding rules to enter a trade can prevent investors from placing orders that deviate from their trading plan. Rules could be created using technical or fundamental analysis, or a combination of both.

- **Be committed to risk management:** Traders who exercise strict position size management tend to outperform those who don't regardless of the systems or time frames being traded. Managing risk on individual trade will also diffuse the likelihood of a large drawdown, in turn reducing the psychological pitfalls that come from such circumstances.

Many traders overtrade when they are bored. They are bored and impatient and put on trade even though they don't have a very good trading idea. They trade on impulse with no specific plan or rationale. It's just something to do. It may not seem like much of a problem but if you do it repeatedly, little losses here and there and commission costs start to add up. In the long run, it is in your best interests to control this impulse.

Risk Management

Risk management helps cut down losses. It can also help protect traders' accounts from losing all its money. The risk occurs when traders suffer losses. If the risk can be managed, traders can open themselves up to making money in the market.

It is an essential but often overlooked prerequisite to successful active trading. A trader who has generated substantial profits can lose it all in just one or two bad trades without a proper risk management strategy. So how do you develop the best techniques to curb the risks of the market?

Stop-loss (S/L) and take-profit (T/P) points represent two key ways in which traders can plan ahead when trading. Successful traders know what price they are willing to pay and at what price they are willing to sell. They can then measure the resulting returns against the probability of the stock hitting their goals. If the adjusted return is high enough, they execute the trade.

Setting Stop-Loss and Take-Profit Points

A stop-loss point is the price at which a trader will sell a stock and take a loss on the trade. This often happens when a trade does not pan out the way a trader hoped. The points are designed to prevent the "it will come back" mentality and limit losses before they escalate. For example, if a stock breaks below a key support level, traders often sell as soon as possible.

On the other hand, a take-profit point is the price at which a trader will sell a stock and take a profit on the trade. This is when the additional upside is limited given the risks. For example, if a stock is approaching a key resistance level after a large move upward, traders may want to sell before a period of consolidation takes place.

A great way to place stop-loss or take-profit levels is on support or resistance trend lines. These can be drawn by connecting previous highs or lows that occurred on significant, above-average volume. The key is determining levels at which the price reacts to the trend lines and, of course, on high volume.

How does a Stop loss and Target level work?

Consider below example of Balarampur Chini

As per our chart, Entry was at 409, first target was at 526.25 with a SL of around 350. This means at the same time when we enter a trade, we must add SL and target also with the possible option available in your broker app.

Adding the SL ensures that your position will be closed off at this position and you must take it as a loss and journal or analyse it further why it didn't go as per your expectations.

There can be multiple targets for a trade setup. E.g., if there are 3 targets, book some when first target is met and now move your stoploss to entry price.

Below is a chart with multiple targets:

Now, we have little hang of what is Support, Resistance, Stoploss and Target.

We are ready to dig deeper into Risk Management.

1-2% rule is very popular within traders which says for any loosing position, a trader must not lose more than 1-2% of his portfolio. E.g., if your portfolio size is of say 10, 00, 000 INR i.e., Rs. 10,00,000 then you must take position in such a way that a failed trade doesn't cost you more than 10, 000 (1% of 10 lakhs). There are variations to this rule though which depends on several factors like:

1. How much of trading experience you have?
2. What is your success rate?
3. What is your control on emotional trading?
4. How much you are fine loosing per trade?
5. What is your control on greed?

If we notice and check above things, it varies from person to person, so if you ask me, it depends but in no case, even in the best-looking trade setup, don't put yourself in such a phase where you are losing more than 4% of your portfolio in one trade. In 4%, I assumed that you are good in trading and good with 5 points mentioned above.

Ok, so I keep it as 2% for me in most of my trades. Start with lowest you can, because there are good chances that in starting out of 1 year, you won't be able to outsmart the market and will have plenty of losing trades. Again, that will depend on how good as a trader you have become. The more you analyse, check charts and the more time you spent with the charts, the chances of you getting luckier will improve because slowly you will start understanding why a particular trade came out this way and what next is coming seeing the past data. Who knows, you outsmart the market 90% of times and people start calling you someone from the future.

Now, say we fix our loss % to 2%, means we aren't ready to lose more than 2% of our portfolio amount per trade, which comes as 20, 000 INR for a 10, 00, 000 INR amount.

Position Sizing:

Say, we want to buy a stock, trading at 4Rs. And for this trade our SL (Stop Loss) is of Rs. 3.

(Buying Price – Stop Loss)/Buying Price.

So, in above example, our SL is of 25%.

Let's calculate with how much quantity you should be buying, so you don't lose more than 2% (20, 000 Rs) of your portfolio

20, 000/25% = 80, 000. So, here you should take the trade with 80, 000 Rs such that even if SL hits, which was at 25%, you won't lose more than 20,000 Rs.

Risk/reward ratio

It also known as the risk/return ratio marks the prospective reward an investor can earn for every dollar they risk on an investment. Many investors use risk/reward ratios to compare the expected returns of an investment with the amount of risk they must undertake to earn these returns.

Consider the following example: an investment with a risk-reward ratio of 1:7 suggests that an investor is willing to risk $1, for the prospect of earning $7. Alternatively, a risk/reward ratio of 1:3 signals that an investor should expect to invest $1, for the prospect of earning $3 on their investment.

To my trades for example, I keep a RR ratio of at least 1. RR of 1 means for a trade, stop loss and Target Price would be equidistant.

Consider, below chart for example,

In above chart, you see Risk Reward ratio of 5. So, if I kept a positional trade with SL of 100$, with this setup, my profit in the trade will be 5*100 = 500 $.

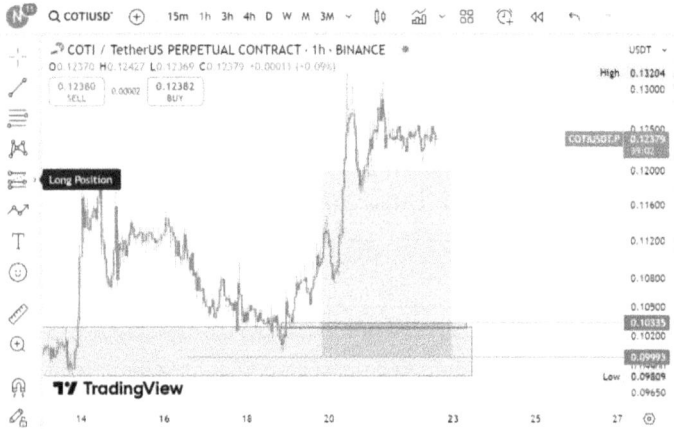

Here, on the left side where you see Long Position, this is the tool in trading view to draw short or long position and to identify your Risk Reward ratio.

Considering you have a success rate of 100% and you have 5RR of Risk Reward ratio of your last 20 trades, then congratulations! You have doubled your money in 20 trades with 1% risk on reach trades. *So, a good RR with a good success ratio is what you want.*

Real - Life examples:

Case studies of successful trades and lessons from losses:

I am going to add some case studies on the type of trades I took, some of which went success and lessons learn from some which didn't go well. You might not be able to understand how I took these trades if you just started your trading journey but for some it would clarify how I took these trades and what to expect in next series of books to come.

AIusdt.p : This is a crypto coin chart with ticker as AIusddt.p

In below chart, in 4HR chart, price took liquidity below at around 0.33359. Did a BMS post that and that taken first liquidity again which is a high probability buy setup as per me.

Drawing all this in a setup will look like as shown in example below. I know it would look a little too complex to understand, that's why I want to move books into the market slowly from time-to-time increasing complexity each time.

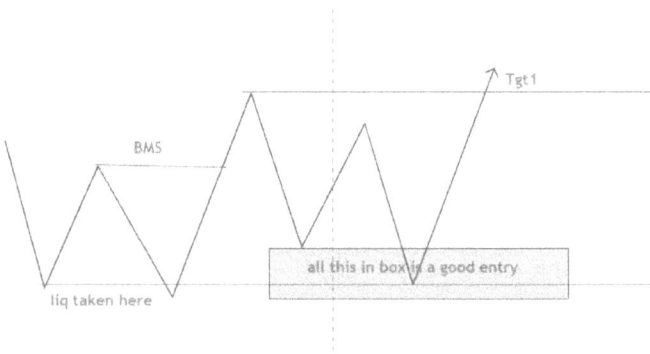

ARBusdt.p: This is a cryto coin chart with ticker as ARusdt.p

See below chart, a similar setup of what was used in AIusdt.p

Notice here, there's mention of a new keyword. Look closely, found it? Yes, EQH. EQH means equal highs. Similarly, we have EQL meaning Equal Lows. They have their meanings, and these are like price magnets, price gets attracted to EQH and EQL prices. But why? Did I mention about liquidity in previous chapters? Yes, these are related to liquidity. When present at highs is called Equal highs and when present at lows are called Equal Lows.

Personal anecdotes

Enough of learning, let's take a break, let me tell you something interesting. Do you know had I listening to my heart I would have made in crores by now. Yes, you got it right. You knew how Bitcoin grew from the ashes to the sky right? So, earlier when I was not a market watcher and didn't use to follow markets too often, it was about my job, my little circle of friends with whom I used to hang out and used to do house parties. Yes, you all can invite me for a party and if you are a decent human, mostly I won't say no 😊. Anyways, So I was by chance looking at financial markets and to my amaze, Bitcoin was trading at around 4.5K dollars. I think I saw it at 7k just a month back. I was like "That's amazing, I should buy it". I remember me asking my mom, "Mom! I want to buy Bitcoin worth Rs. 20L!" and my mom said buy with 1-2 L if you want but not more than that. Anyways, you don't know much about such assets, and these are very volatile. At that time, I didn't know any of technical analysis or how to read charts, neither I was following anyone with good technical analysis. Overall, no cryptos or TA gurus that time. And what has happened in the history, everyone has seen price of Bitcoin where it went to and now where it will go to. I say with no shame whatsoever, that till this date I don't hold any bitcoins, but I do have a regret, had I any market gurus or people good with TA in my list, time would have been a lot different like how it has been. So, learning and knowing always help. I feel inclined to Finance domain each passing day, there's so much to learn from so many fields available. I would advise each one of you to invest in yourself. Knowledge is power and time is money. Try to learn/read something new each passing day and spend your day wisely.

Poems that I used to write:

For some of you, who might be interested in knowing me a little more about me. I am unmarried, yes! 😊 lol :D Rest details could be discussed as we connect. I used to write poems in past, thinking about someone special, thought may be let's add one of the poems out here, so you also get that part of me which I know is nowhere relevant to trading 😐.

Here it goes:

-->

The road which takes us to heaven, where there's just two of us, blooming flowers look so fresh, butterflies around take our breath.

World which never existed, love in its purest form, talks which make us hold, love which grows multi-fold.

The girl I always thought of the life you always sought for, the dreams I always chased, the love you always craved.

Kisses so hard, to leave taste forever, the smell of our skin, which unite us together.

Together we cry, together we hope,

Together we win, together we lose,

Together we dare, together we learn,

Together we kiss, together will love.

The road less travelled, the dreams less chased, the life less lived and the love less made without you!

--->

Conclusion

Encouragement and concluding thoughts:

This is my first book. Never did I imagine that I will be publishing a book in my life. It was a call from universe I believe, and I was being asked to write what I learnt from the market, the good phases, the phases where I broke down and the lessons learnt.

I want all my readers to suggest this book to their friends if they like it, Also, please leave me feedback on where I was wrong or where I should work on. *Your feedback matters a lot to me*!

I think you won't be able to take many calls after reading this book. From my next book, you will be able to take some calls. I am sure the foundation I tried to lay down in this book was necessary before concentrating too much on Technical Analysis.

Trading is like an unknown game where so many aren't to expertise because of not to good informational available. My idea would be to build a community of traders, where we discuss, analyse, take, and execute. My channels handles will be shared with you.

What's Coming Next

What you can expect in next books to come:

- How to read a candle, swing low, swing high and a chart?
- How to read Breakouts, Fake outs?
- More on Ranges, upside, sideways market, and downside markets?
- What is SMS and BMS?
- Some triangle patters, why they work and why they don't?
- Some other patterns, why they work and why they don't?
- Why trendlines work and why they don't?
- Liquidity and its importance?
- Equilibrium?
- Different market cycles like manipulation, expansion, etc.
- How to take trades using SMS and BMS?
- How to take trades in case of breakouts?

- Fibonacci retracement and extensions in more details to decide on the entry and target prices?
- Liquidity pools, order blocks and fair value gaps.
- EMAs and their usage.

www.ingramcontent.com/pod-product-compliance
Lightning Source LLC
LaVergne TN
LVHW061558070526
838199LV00077B/7103